Your doctor can screen your body and tell you what nearly works.

Well, I wouldn't bother carrying an organ donor card.

He will recommend future fitness programmes. . .

Every day?

COLIN WHITTOCK

The Perils of Pushing 40

CENTURY
LONDON SYDNEY AUCKLAND JOHANNESBURG

Copyright © Colin Whittock 1986

All rights reserved

First published in 1986 by Century Hutchinson Ltd,
Brookmount House, 62–65 Chandos Place, Covent Garden,
London WC2N 4NW

Century Hutchinson Australia Pty Ltd,
89–91 Albion Street, Surry Hills,
New South Wales 2010, Australia

Century Hutchinson New Zealand Limited,
PO Box 40–086, Glenfield, Auckland 10, New Zealand

Century Hutchinson South Africa (Pty) Ltd,
PO Box 337, Bergvlei 2012, South Africa

Reprinted 1986, 1987 (twice), 1988, 1989

ISBN 0 7126 1290 4

Filmset by Deltatype,
Ellesmere Port

Printed in Great Britain by Richard Clay Ltd, Bungay, Suffolk

Fit At 40

Medical screening is becoming more common. For a fee. . .

This is just to make sure you're up to reading my fee scale.

and some form of diet.

It's all muscle!

This takes a little time to adjust to. . .

– after all, a good scoff occasionally does nobody any harm.

It seems a pity to waste that potato...

Eventually dieting is worth it.

I must be losing some weight – I can see the scales again!

But beware – keeping fit can make some suspicious.

You're the only senior executive without an ulcer – what's your game?

You can buy a smart new track suit. . .

Speed stripes are extra, sir!

and join the daily club of early morning joggers,

Morning, gents!

**or you may prefer to buy equipment
that allows you to. . .**

exercise at home.

In! – Out! – In! – Out!

And the New You can look to the future with assurance.

Are you sure he passed our medical?

Sex

Sex life continues with a few changes, like no longer needing a headache on Sunday afternoons. . .

Remember to wake daddy in time for tea.

The sight of a firm young body still thrills. . .

Look at that – like two boys fighting under a blanket!

**– but it's odd how a man's sex urge is
so strong. . .**

Must go lads.   *Is it your birthday?*

          On a promise?   *Need any help?*

until he gets into bed.

And often, when the moment is right. . .

I don't feel like reading tonight.

– somehow it isn't!

You're home early tonight!

Delightful unplanned moments still occur. . .

Don't keep saying, 'We used to do it in a mini', and massage my leg!

but don't change the habits of a lifetime,

You've started taking your socks off first – is there another woman?

or that special trust may be lost.

That was the best ever.

The Younger Generation

The children are growing up. . .

– some are at the later stages of school education,

some go to college or university,

*Don't worry, I'd have only wasted it on a new
car or something.*

and some to work.

*I'm going to buy a car, a guitar, a camera,
some clothes and a holiday in the sun. And
from my second month's salary. . .*

Daughters bring home boyfriends,

Watch his hair doesn't damage the furniture. . .

and sons, their girls.

When you've put your eyes back in, say hello to Güdrun. . .

They become fashion conscious. . .

You made it yourself? – I rather hoped you had!

– sometimes with hurtful effect.

Can I borrow your suit tonight, dad?

But if you can remain mates with your children – you've won!

Lend us a fiver, dad, and I'll take you down to the pub!

Pet Pals

Owning a pet in middle age is said by many to be beneficial.

I think this one has chosen us.

Dogs give a friendly welcome. . .

– and can be a great security device.

*Don't worry – if there is somebody
downstairs, the dog will bark.*

But do be careful – pets can cause jealousy.

I remember when you used to talk to me like that.

Some prefer cats. . .

Live and lct live!

but, all in all, their unquestioning loyalty usually helps a person to relax.

If it wasn't for the dog, I wouldn't get any exercise.

The Social Whirl

Men hate going to dances,

*We'd **both** love to come!*

but usually enjoy them.

*I'd like to apologize for the smashing time I
had with you last night.*

After the first few steps. . .

*Don't be silly, of course everyone isn't
looking at us.*

you often spend the rest of the evening on the dance floor

Honestly, we kept being the only two left at the table.

– but do be careful of what you say when dancing to old tunes.

I could have sworn it was you I danced with all night to this.

An invitation out to a meal can be a break. . .

Put your tongue in.

– sometimes.

Tarquin's into Nouvelle Cuisine!

Dress For Success

Your wife's influence is important because she tells the truth.

To prevent you becoming an ageing trendy. . .

occasionally an impulse purchase will be made.

But what doesn't suit some. . .

Our changes in shape have to be accommodated. . .

I used to be 6' before I went bow-legged!

and despite these casual times. . .

Exhibitionist!

the wrong dress can still cause embarrassment.

Dammit! I clearly said it was formal!

If you look after your clothes. . .

57 odd socks! – Do you have a one-legged lover?

you can dress well and avoid looking middle-aged.

The Sporting Hero

Some sportsmen continue playing into their forties.

I don't know how you find the drive to keep playing. . .

It's good for your ego,

You have to admire him, still playing at his age.

if not for your wife's.

Ooooh!. . . Aaargh!. . . Ooooh!. . . Aaargh!. . .

Some sports are more accommodating,

Old? Maybe. But he can turn the ball like a boomerang and knows all the verses of Eskimo Nell!

especially if you pace yourself.

*Don't go scampering any quick singles – I've
just drunk a substantial lunch. . .*

So, reluctantly, you have to recognize those little signs. . .

You thought you had me that time, didn't you?

and consider more leisurely pursuits. . .

After all, it doesn't mean you have to sever all connections with your favourite sport.

I only said you can go, if you promise not to play . . .

The Music Of Time

By now, one has usually developed a broad taste in music. . .

What do you fancy – some Stockhausen, Val Doonican, Ivor Novello or Roland Rat Sings Irving Berlin?

through modern, middle-of-the-road,

**to the odd classical concert on
Radio 3. . .**

though some have invested in the latest equipment.

Now, if you listen carefully, you'll definitely hear Walenovski burp at the end of the cadenza!

The old problem of relating to the children's music remains. . .

I SAID, it's your turn to ask the kids to turn down their music!

despite efforts all round.

But their ability must be encouraged. . .

I hope they succeed soon – I can't afford the electricity.

and eventually, they grow out of it. . .

*Dad, I've discovered a smashing new group
called 'The Beatles'.*

– mercifully.

Away From It All

That would have been £2,000 for five of us!

As the kids usually want to do their own thing, holidays should be cheaper. . .

That would have been £2,000 for five of us!

– well, a little.

Everyone else is going on the school skiing holiday.

I've always wanted a PGL adventure hol.

But it's a great chance – if you can find the fare, living in America will cost me nothing!

It's a worrying time. . .

Did you tell them where to find the will?

You try not to miss them. . .

Don't keep saying, 'The kids would have loved this'.

– but you do eventually get used to being without them. . .

I sald you wouldn't be able to do this if the kids. . . were. . . about!

with just the occasional lapse.

*Of course you haven't wound down yet – you
leap up every time a child calls 'Mummy!'*

Being without the kids gives you the opportunity to try a different holiday,

They say it's the only way to see Corfu...

brings back romantic memories. . .

Shall we start another family before it's too late?

– and over the years you do learn a lot.

*We must be getting more sensible – we
didn't exchange addresses with anyone!*

Late Arrivals

Once the children have been told,

Ahem. . .

they behave quite maturely.

Why didn't you ask me about contraception?

If you think I'm doing all the babysitting. . .

Good grief! I thought you'd given up that sort of thing ages ago.

Everyone joins in the fun. . .

Setting up a nursery. . .

Tender moments are recalled. . .

and friends share the joy.

Occasional comments hurt,

What do you mean, it's all right for grandparents?

but they say the miracle keeps you young. . .

On The Job

The awareness of growing old hits you suddenly. . .

Who qualifies for a gold watch this year, then?

– when the office dolly bird you think fancies you, seeks advice. . .

You remind me of my dad.

You become classed as loyal. . .

A killer gets less. . .

– but loyalty doesn't always pay.

Yes, there are moves afoot that affect you, but I won't spoil your holiday – I'll wait till you return.

And, of course, by now you know everyone in the company. . .

Some do appreciate an experienced hand. . .

We would give it to the others, but we know you'll do it properly.

**and experience helps at tricky times
like the office party. . .**

You are trusted to guide the youngsters. . .

Haven't you done that yet?

– and watch their promotion.

Haven't you done that yet?

The Future